RAJASTHAN: A JOURNEY THROUGH THE LAND OF ROYALS

EXPLORING THE CULTURE AND VIBRANT LANDSCAPES !!

SIDDHESH PRUSTY

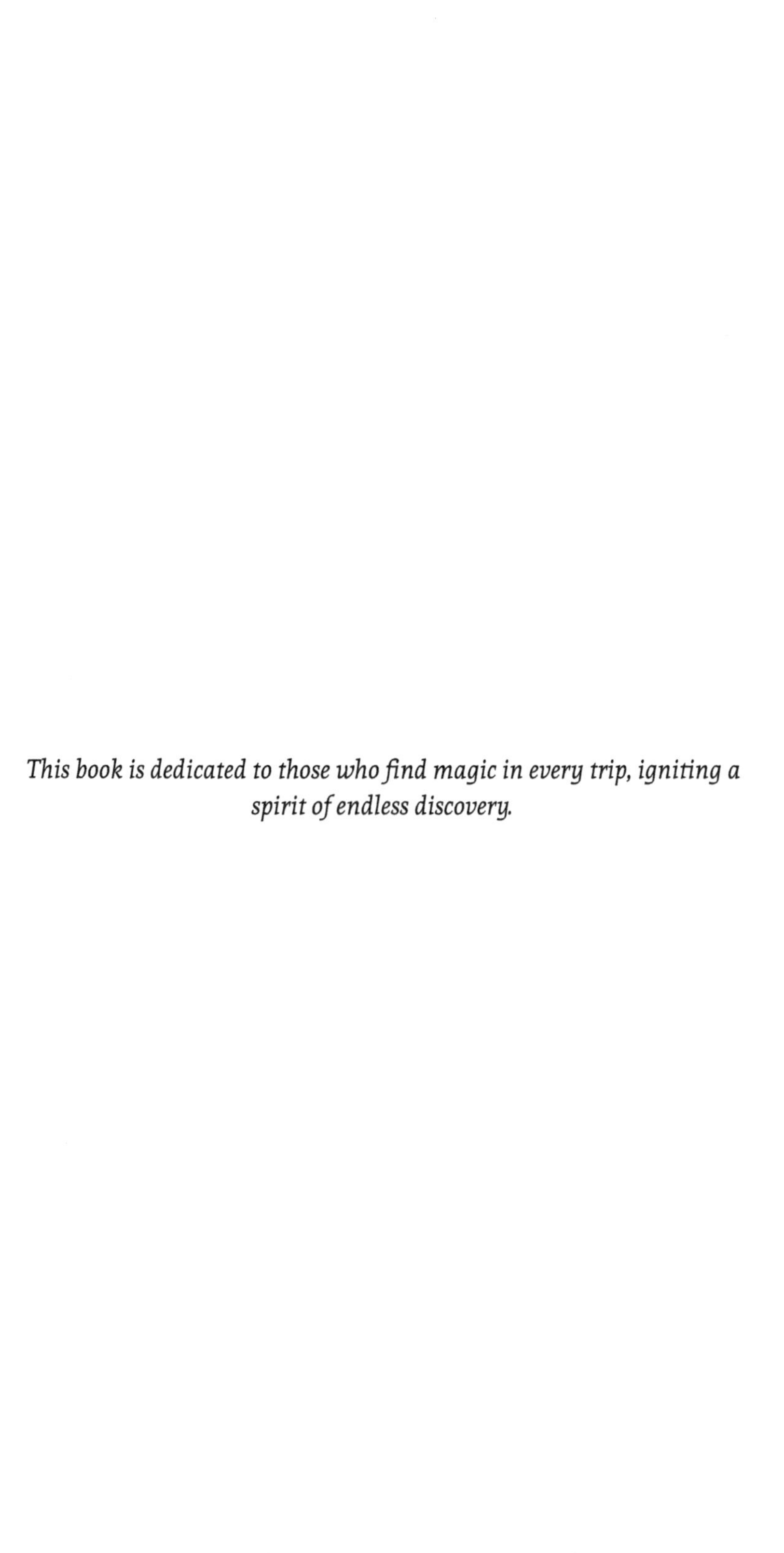

This book is dedicated to those who find magic in every trip, igniting a spirit of endless discovery.

Contents

Foreword

Rajasthan has always been more than a destination—it's a living tapestry of history, culture, and the human spirit. In this book, you will get to wander through the majestic corridors of ancient forts, stroll the colorful lanes of vibrant bazaars, and lose yourself amidst vast, sun-kissed deserts through the point of view of the author.

As you turn these pages, you will feel as though you're stepping back in time, witnessing opulent, regal traditions and immersing yourself in the everyday marvels of Rajasthani life. What Lies Within is not just a travelogue but a heartfelt narrative drawn from personal journeys, unforgettable encounters, and moments of revelation. Each chapter invites you to experience the fusion of history and modernity—a place where festivals light up the night, art adorns the walls of centuries-old palaces, and the spirit of the people transforms every trip into a soulful adventure.

I invite you now to embark on this exploration of wonder, where the legacy of the royals intertwines with the vibrant pulse of everyday life. May this journey inspire you to seek beauty in unexpected places and revel in the magic that resides in every corner of Rajasthan.

— Siddhesh Prusty
Author of "Rajasthan: A Journey Through the Land of Royals"

Preface

I have always been drawn to the vibrant and colorful spirit of Rajasthan—a land where every corner whispers tales of ancient valor and timeless beauty. My journey into its rich history, lively bazaars, and majestic deserts was not just a travel experience but a transformative adventure that awakened a deeper passion for life and culture. Each moment spent amid the bustling streets and serene landscapes of Rajasthan inspired me to capture its essence and share it with you.

1

From Hyderabad to Udaipur: The Royal Journey Commences

The moment I stepped into the bustling Hyderabad airport, a mix of excitement and calm enveloped me. The vast hall, humming with travelers and the sound of hurried announcements, became the canvas upon which I began sketching the tale of my next great adventure. Amid the towering glass walls and shimmering displays, I felt my heart quicken in anticipation—not for the departure itself but for the vibrant experiences that lay ahead in Udaipur and beyond. I was extremely excited for what was about to come in the land of the royals.

Navigating through the organized chaos of check-ins and security, I couldn't help but marvel at how each moment in the airport was a precursor to an unfolding narrative. Walking through the airport, I was struck by the seamless blend of tradition and modernity. The interiors, adorned with intricate artwork, whispered stories of Hyderabad's glorious past—its pearls and its history- while the sleek, contemporary design showcased the city's forward-looking spirit as well as its technological advancements. The spaciousness of the terminals, bathed in natural light, gave a sense of calm amidst the inevitable rush of travelers.

Every piece of luggage, every hurried conversation, and every fleeting smile from fellow travelers were silent reminders that journeys have their unique rhythm. Seated comfortably by the large window at the departure lounge, I spent a few moments absorbing the flow of emotions that travel invariably brings. I recalled previous adventures and imagined the intricate palaces, the sprawling lakes, and the ancient tales of courage and romance that awaited me in Rajasthan. At the same time, I also wondered if Rajasthan was only a desert or if it was a place that awakened minds.

While Hyderabad had been a fitting start to my day with its modern vibrancy and historic charm, I was eager to let ***Udaipur's legendary aura*** sweep me off my feet. The very thought of landing in a city famously nicknamed the "City of Lakes" stirred a deep sense of excitement within me. I wondered about the unique experiences that Udaipur would offer—a chance to step into a narrative woven from centuries-old traditions and modern-day revelry. Every minute spent in the air felt like a gentle reminder of life's transient beauty and the endless opportunities hidden in every destination.

Modern interiors of the Rajiv Gandhi International Airport(Hyderabad)

Boarding the flight, my eyes wandered to the large windows as we ascended gracefully into the sky. As the landscape below shrank to a patchwork of busy cities and farmlands, my thoughts turned exploratory.

As the plane began its descent toward Udaipur, the landscape below transformed into a beautiful painting—a blend of lush greens, sparkling lakes, and hints of a desert's dull charm. The approach was gentle yet exhilarating, offering a sneak peek into the romance of Rajasthan. Udaipur Airport, though small in size compared to mega-hubs, had an undeniable charm that spoke of the city it served. There, modernity met an old-world sense of grace, setting the perfect stage for the journey that awaited.

Standing at the arrival hall, I felt the energy of Udaipur surge through me. My thoughts raced with plans for the hours ahead: maybe a quick jaunt to savor authentic Rajasthani cuisine or a brief exploration into the nearby markets to soak in the local rhythm. *Every idea felt like a spark, igniting a curiosity to capture the essence of this unique city.*

2

Day 1: Touchdown, Check-In, and the Temple Awaits

The day began with excitement as I arrived in the enchanting city of Udaipur and checked into the magnificent Club Mahindra Resort.

Club Mahindra, Udaipur

The resort, with its impeccable service and stunning architecture, immediately set the tone for what was to become an unforgettable experience. The lobby exuded a warm, soothing ambiance with tasteful décor that celebrated both modern comfort and traditional Rajasthani artistry. I was greeted with genuine smiles from the staff and the subtle scent of marigolds and incense, which seemed to whisper promises of a delightful journey ahead.

After settling into my room and savoring a brief moment of repose amidst luxurious surroundings, I marked my itinerary for that day's adventure. I stepped out of the serene retreat of Club Mahindra, energized by the idea of immersing myself in the heart and soul of Udaipur.

My first destination was the revered Karni Mata Mandir, a temple known for its spiritual significance and tranquil atmosphere. The journey from the resort to Karni Mata Mandir was nothing short of captivating.

As I traversed the vibrant streets of Udaipur, the city's pulse revealed itself in every miniature detail. Upon reaching Karni Mata Mandir, I was immediately enveloped by a serene energy that felt both timeless and personal. The temple, dedicated to the revered goddess Karni Mata, was a sanctuary imbued with centuries of devotion and mystique. Its ancient walls, adorned with intricate carvings and traditional motifs, told tales of past reverence and continued faith. I found a quiet corner near the entrance and took a moment to absorb the divine ambiance.

The temple's history dates back to the 15th century, when Karni Mata, a spiritual leader and revered sage, was believed to have performed miracles and guided the local rulers. She was a prominent figure in the Mewar dynasty, and her divine influence is deeply etched in the region's cultural tapestry.

Refreshed and vibing after my temple visit, I said peace out to the chill Karni Mata Mandir vibes and hopped into the next epic chapter—***Lake Pichola***.

Lake Pichola

Cruising back through Udaipur's lit streets, I got all the feels of being drawn to this iconic flex, celebrated for centuries as the mirror of the city's soul. No cap, Lake Pichola was straight-up fire under the playful afternoon sun, its surface a dazzling tapestry of vibrant blue and golden hues.

Once at the lake, I was all in for soaking up its chill vibes by hopping on a boat ride. My dad quickly signed up for a paid boating service, where a captain took the helm, ensuring a smooth ride as we glided across the serene waters. The gentle splash of waves against the hull became the ultimate, rhythmic jam—each ripple sparking a memory, a catchy tune, or a whispered promise of adventure.

By the time the journey on the lake reached its zenith, the sun had begun its graceful descent toward the horizon. I positioned myself at the boat's edge, eager to witness the famed Udaipur sunset, a sight spoken of in hushed, reverent tones. As the golden orb dipped lower, the sky exploded into a breathtaking palette of oranges, pinks, purples, and soft indigos. The setting sun cast vibrant rays across the lake, igniting every ripple with a brilliant, almost magical glow.

Returning to the resort later that evening, I felt a quiet satisfaction—a serene acknowledgment of a day filled with discovery, reflection, and pure, unadulterated joy. The experiences of that afternoon, from the reflective solitude at the ancient temple to the communal marvel of the sunset on the lake, encapsulated the magic of Udaipur.

After a soul-satisfying boat ride on Lake Pichola, resplendent with golden ripples from the setting sun, our adventure took a delightful turn towards the vibrant heart of Udaipur. We began our journey back from the lake, our spirits high and our minds buzzing with memories of the magical water-bound escapade. As we navigated the lively streets on the way to Gangaur Ghat, every turn and every sound felt like an invitation to immerse ourselves deeper into Udaipur's rich cultural tapestry.

The ghat, adorned with colorful steps and locals busy with their daily rituals, felt like the heartbeat of the city. The rhythmic sound of water lapping against the steps blended with the distant tunes of folk music, creating an atmosphere full of life and tradition. There were many other people gathered there just to enjoy the scenery around there.

Our family, filled with excitement, strolled along the ghats, soaking in the essence of Udaipur. We also took many beautiful photos. We decided to inquire about the famous cultural events at Bagore Ki Haveli, a place we'd heard of for **its mesmerizing dance and puppet shows**. The friendly locals at the haveli shared details about the next day's performances, and we eagerly planned to attend, knowing we were in for an unforgettable cultural experience.

Resort Rhapsody: A Night of Puppet Shows, Folk Dances, and Rajasthani Delights

With our hearts full of anticipation for a day of further cultural revelry, we gradually made our way back to our sanctuary—the magnificent Club Mahindra Hotel in Udaipur. We freshened up, our minds buzzing with excitement for the cultural extravaganza we were about to witness. The hotel organized a special in-house cultural evening to cap off our first day in Udaipur. This carefully curated event embraced the true essence of Rajasthani art—an amalgamation of lively folk dance, an endearing puppet show, and a sumptuous feast that celebrated the state's culinary prowess.

Firstly, there was an exquisite puppet show—a delightful miniature theater of stories. The puppeteer's nimble fingers brought to life a cast of intricately crafted puppets, each with its personality and charm. The puppets enacted timeless tales of heroism, wit, and romance, their playful interactions evoking both laughter and wonder among the crowd. I found myself completely absorbed in the quirky narratives, marveling at how these tiny figures could encapsulate the grandeur of Rajasthani lore with such finesse.

Complementing the puppet show were the traditional Rajasthani dances. According to what I know, Rajasthan is a land of vibrant traditions and rich cultural heritage and is home to numerous folk dances, each with a unique history and symbolic significance, so I expected a lot from their cultural dance. Among the most captivating are **Ghoomar** and **Kalbeliya**, as well as the intriguing dances involving pots, such as **Pot Dance (Bhavai Dance)** and **Fire Dance.**

I witnessed **the Fire Dance.** It's a mesmerizing performance where dancers balance pots filled with burning flames on their heads. It is performed over burning embers, known as "matire," and where these embers are burned is known locally as **Dhuna**, hence the name "fire dance."This dance has a spiritual and ritualistic significance, often performed during religious ceremonies and festivals. The fire symbolizes purity, energy, and the divine presence. The dancers' movements are bold and rhythmic, with the flames representing the dancers' inner strength and courage. I was shocked to watch such a spectacular dance.

Rajasthani Fire Dance

Next, there was the **Pot Dance**, also known as the Bhavai Dance, which was an energetic performance where dancers balanced multiple clay pots on their heads. This dance is popular among the tribal communities of Rajasthan. The pots, it seems, symbolized prosperity, fertility, and the importance of water in the desert landscape. The dancers, dressed in traditional attire with vibrant turbans and jewelry, perform rhythmic movements, showcasing their balance, strength, and coordination. In essence, this dance comprises female dancers dancing while supporting 8 or 9 pitchers on their heads.

In this nerve-wracking, suspenseful dance, the skilful dancers balance several clay pots or brass figurines before swaying while ***resting the soles of their feet on the top of broken pieces of glass, occasionally on the edge of a bare sword or sometimes on the rim of a brass thali, which let me tell you is extremely hard.*** The dance was historically performed during harvest festivals to celebrate the abundance of crops and the community's agricultural success.

Rajasthani Pot Dance with 9 pots

Lastly, they ended the cultural event with **Ghoomar,** a traditional folk dance performed by women, characterized by graceful, circular movements. It's usually performed in Rajasthan's weddings and festive gatherings. Dancers wear colorful ghagras (long skirts) with intricate embroidery and mirror work, paired with odhnis (scarves) that flow elegantly as they spin. The dance symbolizes joy, celebration, and community bonding. Looks like their dance did rise above my expectations, and I was extremely impressed on seeing it.

Both the Pot Dance and Fire Dance showcase Rajasthan's rich folk traditions, reflecting the region's connection to nature, spirituality, and the celebratory spirit of its people.

Then came the grand finale—a sumptuous dinner featuring an authentic Rajasthani thali that was nothing short of a culinary masterpiece. The thali arrived as an artful mosaic of dishes: vibrant curries spiced just right, freshly made rotis, aromatic rice, tangy chutneys, and a delightful assortment of savory snacks.

Some items in the Rajasthani cuisine include Tawa Fish, Laal Maas(Mutton), Dal Bati Churma, and Ghevar(a traditional Rajasthani sweet). Each component of the thali was a burst of flavor, reflecting the rich, diverse culinary traditions of Rajasthan. Every bite told a story, and I couldn't help but relish the way the spices danced on my tongue, perfectly complementing the cultural feast our eyes had feasted upon earlier.

As we sat together around the table, sharing stories of our evening escapades and laughing over local jokes, the comfortable glow of the hotel's dining area wrapped us in a sense of serene togetherness. The animated discussions about the mesmerizing folk dance, the clever antics of the puppets, and our shared delight over the authentic flavors made it clear that the day had been far more than just an itinerary—it had already become an emotional journey filled with connection and celebration.

Every moment of that night, from the friendly greetings at the hotel to the soulful performances on the stage, reinforced just how special our first day in Udaipur had been. It was a seamless blend of culture, art, and family bonding—a reminder that travel isn't only about visiting new places but about experiencing the heart and soul of each destination.

The evening's cultural extravaganza had transformed our return to the club into an affirmation of the rich traditions that make Rajasthan so captivating.

In the soft afterglow of the night's festivities, I retired to my room with my family still laughing and reminiscing about the Pot dance and the Fire dance.

3

Day 2: Udaipur Odyssey: Exploring City Palace, Bagore Ki Haveli, Jagdish Mandir & Savoring a Gujarati Thali

The day started on a high note at Club Mahindra Hotel, where we enjoyed a ***sumptuous breakfast buffet*** that delighted our taste buds and lifted our spirits. Fresh, flaky croissants melted in our mouths alongside steaming cups of coffee, while an enticing mix of South Indian favorites—dosas, idlis, and vadas—sat alongside North Indian staples like parathas and poha.

The breakfast wasn't merely a meal; it was a flavorful prelude that filled us with energy and excitement for the adventures awaiting us.

After we savored every bite of that mouthwatering food, we decided to set out a little earlier than usual (about 9:00 a.m.)to make the most of our day. As the first light of dawn painted the sky in soft pinks and oranges, we stepped out of the hotel with cameras in hand and hearts full of anticipation.

The early morning air was crisp and invigorating, perfectly complementing our eagerness to explore the famed **City Palace of Udaipur.**

Udaipur's City Palace

The journey to the City Palace was a delightful experience in itself. The tranquility of the morning allowed us to fully appreciate the intricate details of the surrounding architecture and the gentle ambiance of a city rich in history. With each step, we felt the promise of the past, and as we neared our destination, the majestic silhouette of the City Palace emerged against the backdrop of the awakening sky.

City Palace, with its sprawling courtyards, ornate corridors, and stunning blend of art and architecture, was a sight to behold. As we wandered through its grand halls, the palace's rich tapestries of intricate carvings, vibrant murals, and delicate lattice work unfolded before our eyes.

Each structure, every artifact, and every carefully painted fresco told a story of royal legacy and timeless elegance. *We couldn't resist pausing frequently to capture these moments with our cameras—each*

click preserving a fraction of the awe and inspiration we felt.

Built in the mid-16th century by Maharana Udai Singh II—the very founder of Udaipur—the palace began its majestic journey as the royal residence of the Mewar dynasty.

Over the centuries, successive rulers added their unique touches, transforming the initially modest structure into a sprawling complex that masterfully blends Rajput fortification with Mughal opulence.

Today, the City Palace stands as a living museum, a cultural treasure where the spirit of the past is lovingly preserved. The ***present king of Mewar, Maharana Bhupal Singh***, continues this legacy with deep reverence for his ancestors.

His active efforts in cultural preservation and heritage promotion have ensured that the intricate mosaic of traditions, art, and history remains accessible to visitors worldwide.

Under his guidance, the palace is not merely a relic of history but a vibrant center where the living traditions of the Mewar dynasty continue to inspire and educate.

As one wanders through the palace's grand halls, the walls come alive with a vivid collection of paintings that capture the soul of Rajasthan. Stunning miniature paintings are also present there. These artworks are more than just decorative; each piece serves as a visual document of a rich cultural narrative, depicting renowned figures such as Maharana Pratap and capturing the regal ceremonies of the era.

One of the exquisite paintings featured in City Palace

Beyond the paintings, the palace is a veritable treasure trove of artifacts that narrate stories of a bygone era. Antique armory, including ***intricately designed swords and shields,*** sit alongside ornate jewelry, royal garments, and ceremonial regalia that showcase the wealth and sophistication of the Mewar court. Each artifact, from carved furniture to gilded mirrors, is a testament to the exquisite craftsmanship and aesthetic sensibilities of the time. A particularly captivating exhibit is the display of ancient manuscripts and scrolls.

The beautifully designed walls of the City Palace

Visiting City Palace is an immersive experience. As you pass through its corridors and expansive galleries, the harmonious blend of history, art, and royal legacy envelops you. The palace is far more than an architectural marvel; it is a dynamic storyteller that bridges the gap between the pages of history and the present day. Under the custodianship of Maharana Bhupal Singh, this iconic monument continues to celebrate and preserve the illustrious legacy of Mewar, inviting every visitor to relive the vibrant tapestry of its royal past.

The early morning light danced beautifully on the palace's walls and domes, creating fleeting patterns of shadow and brilliance. These artistic contrasts accentuated the beauty of every arch and column, making our photography a vibrant reflection of the scene before us. We took our time meandering through the various sections of the City Palace, from the echoing halls that housed centuries-old treasures to the peaceful terraces that offered a panoramic view of Udaipur's historic landscape.

By the time we wrapped up our visit, our cameras were brimming with photos that captured not only the stunning architecture of the City Palace but also the joy and wonder of the morning. The memories we created in that serene slice of Udaipur were a perfect blend of culinary delight, cultural exploration, and unbridled family fun.

After an immersive morning exploring the grandeur of the City Palace, we slowly stepped out, our hearts still echoing with tales of regal legacy and meticulous craftsmanship. The vibrant corridors and sprawling courtyards slowly faded into the distance as we left one of Udaipur's most iconic landmarks.

With smiles still playing on our lips from the memorable journey through history, our next destination was the city's famous ***wax museum***—a quirky yet fascinating detour.

Stepping into the wax museum, we were immediately greeted by an array of lifelike figures that blurred the line between art and reality. It was as if history and modern celebrity had merged into one spectacular exhibit. From renowned personalities to legendary figures of the past, every wax statue was meticulously crafted, capturing the essence and expressions of its subject perfectly.

We lingered, snapping selfies and marveling at the artistry behind each creation, our laughter and excited chatter filling the bright, gallery-like space.

After taking in the surreal spectacle of the wax figures, our growing appetites nudged us onward to one of Udaipur's culinary treasures—a famous sweet shop known as ***Jagdish Misthan Bhandar***.

The moment we stepped inside, the rich scent of sweetness and spice embraced us like a warm welcome. We couldn't resist indulging in the local favorite: the world-famous Rajasthani *pyaz kachori*, which was irresistibly crunchy on the outside and bursting with a tangy, aromatic filling that was piping hot.

Alongside, we savored the traditional *Ghevar*— a traditional Rajasthani sweet that is popular during festivals like Teej and Raksha Bandhan.

It is made from a batter of flour, ghee, and milk, which is deep-fried and then soaked in sugar syrup. Ghevar has a unique lacy and honeycomb-like texture and is often garnished with nuts, saffron, and cardamom that melts in our mouths—complemented by a serving of *dhokla and vibrant green chutney*, each bite delivering an authentic taste of Rajasthani—and indeed, regional—culinary magic.

Ghevar

Pyaz Kachori

With our taste buds delightfully satisfied, we set off once again, our spirits buoyed by the promise of more cultural festivities. We headed back to **Bagore Ki Haveli,** where the prior night's excitement had been only a glimpse of what awaited.

The tickets we had prebooked the previous day filled us with anticipation for another round of spectacular performances. At the haveli, the ambience was truly electric: Traditional Rajasthani music floated through the air, mingling with laughter and applause as elegant dancers twirled on stage.

The puppet show, with its intricate storytelling and expressive miniature figures, added a playful charm to the evening, ensuring that every member of our family was swept up in the cultural celebration.

Not wanting the cultural tour of Udaipur to end there, our footsteps then led us to the majestic **Jagdish Mandir.** The temple's towering spires and intricately carved facades stood as a testament to centuries of devotion and architectural ingenuity.

In the soft glow of the evening, the temple's indelible beauty was highlighted, inviting us to pause and absorb its serene atmosphere. We marveled at the fine details—each pillar and sculpted relief a silent ode to the skills of ancient craftsmen.

Jagdish Mandir

Finally, after a day filled with art, history, and culinary delights, we concluded our adventure at Nataraj Restaurant. Here, we relished a sumptuous Gujarati thali featuring items such as ker sangri, mini kachori, and paratha, along with a wide variety of curries and bhajis — a perfect medley of flavors that harmoniously blended tangy, spicy, and sweet notes into a satisfying meal. Every dish on the thali narrated its own story, making our dinner a fitting finale to a day steeped in the rich traditions of Udaipur. Let me tell you **the food was delicious....(trying to make you jealous, hehe).**

Gujarati Thali at Nataraj

With full hearts and contented smiles, we then made our way back to Club Mahindra Hotel, carrying with us the vibrant memories of a day that had showcased the best of Udaipur—from iconic monuments and quirky museums to lively cultural performances and delightful eats.

END OF CHAPTER 2

4

Day 3: A Journey through the divine heritage pilgrimage

We left our Club Mahindra Hotel at around 12:30 p.m., our hearts full of anticipation and excitement for the day's spiritual and cultural exploration. The early afternoon sun was high and mellow as we embarked on our journey toward **Shrinathji Temple**, a revered landmark known for its tranquil atmosphere and deep-rooted spiritual heritage.

As we navigated the bustling roads, our route took us along the main road of **Haldighati**—a place steeped in history and natural wonder. There, amid the rhythmic flow of traffic and the hum of daily life, we paused to marvel at a truly unique sight: golden brown particles gently emerging from the rock.

The natural phenomenon caught our eyes as the sunlight danced upon them, creating a mesmerizing display that felt almost otherworldly—a subtle reminder of nature's magic woven within the very fabric of this ancient land. Haldighati is named after the yellow-colored soil of the region, which resembles turmeric, known as "haldi" in Hindi.

The area is also famous for the Battle of Haldighati, a significant historical event.

Haldighati

Continuing, we soon arrived at Shrinathji Temple. The temple's serene environment and meticulously preserved architecture brought an immediate sense of calm.

We took our time, savoring the spiritual energy that permeated the sacred space, its walls imbued with echoes of centuries of devotion and tradition.

From Shrinathji Temple, our journey led us to Vishwas Swaroopam, also commonly known as the Statue of Belief. Here, an exquisitely crafted statue awaited us—its divine expression and intricate detailing a perfect blend of artistry and spirituality.

The statue, celebrated for its serene yet commanding presence, featured delicate carvings that highlighted every nuance of traditional craftsmanship.

The 'Statue of Belief' is an awe-inspiring **369-foot-tall artwork of Lord Shiva located in Nathdwara, Rajasthan**. It is one of the largest Shiva statues in the world and among the five largest statues worldwide.

Vishwas Swaroopam(Statue of Beleif)

I was amazed looking at his marvelous piece of art.

Our next stop was the famous Eklingji Temple, known not only as a center of religious reverence but also as an architectural marvel. As we approached the temple, we were instantly captivated by its graceful design. The intricate stone carvings, towering spires, and expansive courtyards spoke of a bygone era when art and spirituality were intertwined seamlessly.

Inside, the calm and sacred ambience provided the perfect setting for prayer, reflection, and a deep appreciation of centuries-old traditions. We marveled at the meticulous workmanship and the harmonious blend of form and function, each element echoing the devotion that inspired its creation.

After spending a reflective and fulfilling time at Eklingji Temple, we retraced our steps and began our journey back to Club Mahindra Hotel. The evening had crept in gracefully as we navigated the scenic roads, our minds still echoing with the day's wondrous experiences.

Our return was bittersweet—filled with the satisfaction of having enriched our spirits through these encounters, yet tinged with the excitement of the next chapter on our journey, as we prepared to travel by bus to Jaisalmer later that evening.

By the time we reached our hotel, the sky was painted with the soft hues of dusk. We were content, grateful for a day that had unfolded like a spiritual tapestry—each moment, from the golden glow of Haldighati to the divine artistry of Vishwas Swaroopam and the architectural splendor of Eklingji Temple, had added another vibrant thread to our travel story. With our hearts full and preparations in place for the next adventure, we settled in for the evening, cherishing the day's memories and eagerly anticipating the journey ahead.

Exhausting Yet Memorable: Our AC Odyssey from Udaipur to Jaisalmer

After our soulful exploration of Eklingji Temple, we slowly made our way back to Club Mahindra Hotel in the gentle embrace of the evening. The temple's grandeur and the spiritual energy we had absorbed lingered in our minds as we drove along in the fading light of dusk. Once we reached the hotel, the first order of business was to pack up our clothes and personal belongings. There was a palpable mix of excitement and a touch of nostalgia as we stowed away our memories of the day, knowing that a new chapter awaited us in Jaisalmer.

With our bags neatly packed and a plan in place for the next leg of our journey, we set our sights on the bus ride to Jaisalmer. Our journey was scheduled to begin at 9:30 p.m. with an AC bus—a modern, comfortable means of travel that promised a break from the heat and a relatively smooth ride through the changing landscapes of Rajasthan. Despite the promise of air-conditioned comfort, the long haul ahead was clear: a journey that would stretch until 7:40 a.m. the next morning, requiring us to navigate almost ten hours on the road.

At 9:30 p.m., under a starlit sky that hinted at the adventures still to come, we set off from our hotel towards the bus station. The cool evening air was refreshing, and the city lights of Udaipur sparkled softly as we boarded our AC bus. Settling into our seats, we could feel the hum of the engine and the gentle buzz of the air conditioner—a promise of temporary solace from the relentless Rajasthan heat. As the bus pulled away from the station, the city gradually receded, replaced by the vast openness of the roads leading toward the desert landscape.

Inside the vehicle, the environment was cool and relatively comfortable, fostering small conversations and moments of quiet reflection.

Outside, however, the scenery evolved from the vibrant urban mosaic of Udaipur into wide, open highways flanked by stretches of arid land and sparse vegetation. While the comfortable seats and air conditioning enhanced our ride, the long hours chipped away at our energy, and by the time midnight neared, fatigue was beginning to set in.

Just when I was about to go into the world of dreams, at around 12:30 a.m., the bus made an unscheduled stop at a bustling dhaba—a lively, open-air roadside eatery that had transformed into a temporary hub for weary travelers.

The dhaba was teeming with energy; several buses had halted along the same stretch, and the place buzzed with a mix of road warriors, families, and solo adventurers, all sharing a momentary respite from their long journeys.

The aroma of freshly made food mingled with laughter and animated chatter in the cool night air, creating an atmosphere that was both rustic and warmly inviting.

Eager for a break from the monotony of the long ride and the lingering exhaustion, we decided to stretch our legs and join in the communal spirit of the stop. In a delightful twist of fun amidst the fatigue, we opted for something unexpected—**ice cream**.

Yes, at that nearly magical hour, we treated ourselves to some ice cream, the rich flavors adding a burst of sweetness to our otherwise weariness.

As we savored **each cold, creamy bite** (wanna make it tempting), the shared delight over this simple pleasure resonated with everyone around us. Conversations flowed as effortlessly as the refreshments, and the collective experience of stopping for a dhaba break turned into a cheerful episode that eased the weariness of our journey.

After our ice cream break and some hearty conversations with fellow travelers, the bus resumed its route. Back in the cool confines of the air-conditioned cabin, the journey continued under the watchful eyes of a dark, starry sky punctuated by the occasional lights from distant settlements.

The later hours were quieter—many passengers rested, lulled by the rhythmic vibrations of the bus and the soft hum of the AC. Despite the comfort technology provided, the endurance required by such a lengthy journey was palpable.

The constant motion combined with long stretches of solitude eventually left us feeling both reflective and thoroughly exhausted, yet there were beds installed in the bus, so we tried to get as much rest as possible.

As the bus neared its destination, the gradual lightening of the sky signaled that our nocturnal journey was coming to a close. By 7:40 a.m., we finally arrived in Jaisalmer—a city that promised new wonders and adventures with its golden hues and storied past. While the bus journey had been far from luxurious, it was a significant chapter in our travel narrative: a blend of comfort provided by modern amenities and the inherent challenges of long-distance travel.

The exhaustion we felt was punctuated by moments of unexpected joy, like that delightful dhaba stop and our sweet ice cream indulgence, which offered small yet memorable pauses in an otherwise continuous journey.

In respect, the evening return to our hotel and the subsequent bus ride encapsulated the spirit of traveling in Rajasthan—a mixture of preparation, the pragmatics of packing, and the raw, unfiltered experiences on the road. As we stepped off the bus in Jaisalmer, we carried with us not only our packed belongings but also the rich sequence of memories from an exhausting yet rewarding journey, ready to embrace the magic of the **Golden City.**

5

Day 4: Wondering what's Golden City? Let me show you!

———❦———

At around 8:00 a.m. the next day, our journey culminated in the arrival at Golden City. Have you been asking yourself what the Golden City is? Well, The Golden City, also known as *Jaisalmer*, is located in the heart of the Thar Desert, Rajasthan. Its name, "Golden City," derives from its **distinct sandstone architecture**, which shines brilliantly under the desert sun, especially during sunrise and sunset.

This golden glow is most evident in the city's magnificent forts, palaces, and havelis, which are built from yellow sandstone, giving the entire city an ethereal, almost magical appearance.

Stepping off the bus into the soft, early morning light, we were immediately struck by the stark beauty of the landscape.

After a brief wait for our luggage, we hailed a taxi that took us along winding roads flanked by these barren fields. Stretching alongside the road were vast, bare fields, completely devoid of any vegetation. The arid expanse, with its dust and scattered golden hues, painted a picture of raw, untouched nature—a dramatic contrast to the bustling scenes of urban life we had known.

The endless openness of the desert landscape created an atmosphere of quiet contemplation where every moment felt both isolating and extraordinarily beautiful. The simplicity of the surroundings, where the earth and sky merged into one uninterrupted canvas, served as a gentle prelude to what was awaiting us at the hotel.

Our destination, the Club Mahindra Hotel in Jaisalmer, loomed in the distance like a majestic oasis. From the outside, the hotel's architecture was nothing short of breathtaking. The facade was a wonderful melding of traditional Rajasthani design and modern elegance.

Interiors of Club Mahindra in Jaisalmer

Exterior view

Its sandstone walls, carved with intricate, ornate patterns reminiscent of ancient forts, shone in the early morning sunlight. Arched doorways and decorative balconies added to the regal allure, making the hotel appear as though it was a part of the desert's natural splendor—a timeless monument standing proudly amid the harsh yet enchanting landscape.

Entering the hotel, we were welcomed into an equally impressive interior. The grand lobby echoed the architectural elegance seen on the exterior, with spacious, well-lit corridors adorned with rich textiles and subtle nods to Rajasthan's cultural heritage. One of the highlights was the stunning swimming pool—a crystalline haven where the water shimmered under meticulously arranged lighting. This pool provided a refreshing contrast to the rugged desert outside, inviting guests to relax and unwind.

Adjacent to the pool, we discovered the hotel's very own "Happy Hub"—a delightful recreational area designed to offer a variety of indoor sports and leisure activities. Here, the atmosphere was lively and spirited. Guests were engaged in energetic matches of air hockey and friendly rounds of chess, while others immersed themselves in video games on a PS5 or enjoyed a casual game of billiards. It also had a shop featuring traditional Rajasthani sarees.

The cheerful buzz in this area, combined with comfortable seating and contemporary decor, created a perfect setting for both relaxation and a bit of fun competition. It was clear that every detail of the interior was thoughtfully designed to ensure that guests experienced the best of modern amenities without losing touch with the rich cultural context of Jaisalmer.

The contrast between the barren fields outside and the inviting, opulent interiors of the Club Mahindra Hotel was striking. While the desert exuded a timeless, rugged charm, the hotel provided a warm, luxurious retreat where every corner was infused with beauty and modern comforts.

At that moment, arriving in Jaisalmer felt not only like the start of a new adventure in a city steeped in history and culture but also like a welcome return to a space where relaxation and recreation awaited, perfectly bridging the gap between the ancient desert and contemporary living.

Desert Delights: A Family Jeep Safari, Camel Ride, Dance, and Authentic Rajasthani Feast

Below is the story of our family adventure—a day we had long dreamed about, and finally booked as an all-in-one package, complete with a thrilling jeep safari over sand dunes, a gentle camel ride through the desert, mesmerizing Rajasthani dance performances (including the pot dance and the fire dance) with soulful songs, and culminating in an authentic Rajasthani feast featuring the region's legendary dishes.

This is the narrative of how my family and I plunged into this unforgettable experience, savoring each moment with pure joy, wonder, and a good measure of light-hearted fun.

It all began with a spark of excitement on a quiet afternoon at our Club Mahindra hotel. We had been discussing the possibility of exploring the desert in Jaisalmer—a destination known for its golden landscapes. The idea of a package that bundled a jeep safari, camel ride, mesmerizing folk performances, and an authentic Rajasthani dinner was simply irresistible.

We decided to book the package via the travel desk present in the hotel. The person present at the travel desk walked us through various packages, explaining in simple words what each activity entailed.

I was very much excited at the mention of riding through the vast, shimmering dunes in a sturdy jeep. The agent even demonstrated small video clips of previous groups laughing, dancing, and feasting under the starlit sky. We knew we had to book that package.

After a few formalities and an easy payment process, our booking was confirmed. The package promised a day filled with a series of exhilarating adventures and cultural experiences. We left the travel agent's office feeling giddy with anticipation, our minds already brimming with images of endless sand dunes, vibrant dances, and mouthwatering food.

The stage was set for adventure: by the time the sun dipped low in the sky, we would be fully equipped and ready to embark on our thrilling desert escapade. Excitement buzzed in the air as we prepared for the journey ahead!

Then it was time to board a robust, open-top jeep specially arranged for the safari. Stepping into the jeep felt a bit like climbing into the cockpit of an adventure machine. The seats were comfortable and a little worn, a testament to the many journeys this jeep had taken across the desert.

We set off slowly, the soft light of dawn turning the horizon into hues of pastel pinks and oranges. As we drove away from the desert camp, the city gradually faded into the background, replaced by the vast, undulating expanse of the desert. I remember how the jeep's engine rumbled in a steady, soothing cadence, as though echoing the heartbeat of the desert itself.

Soon, we reached the beginning of the sand dunes. The golden sands stretched out like an endless ocean, their curves rising and falling in waves that glistened under the setting sun. Our guide skillfully steered the jeep over the dunes, and soon we were riding high atop the crests of these natural hills. My family's laughter filled the air—each bump in the road was met with delight.

I took turns capturing these moments with our camera. We snapped photo after photo—the jeep against a backdrop of rolling sand.

The simple thrill of being in the middle of such raw nature, surrounded by nothing but the vastness of the desert, filled us with a sense of freedom and wonder.

During the safari, our guide pointed out interesting features of the landscape and explained how the patterns in the sand were formed by winds that had been sculpting the dunes for centuries.

His words, delivered in simple language, made us appreciate the subtle artistry of nature.

Every moment on that jeep ride was a blend of excitement and tranquility, the adrenaline of riding over the unpredictable dunes perfectly balanced by the peaceful, endless horizon before us.

Once the jeep safari had taken its course and we had savored that exquisite taste of adventure on wheels, the next experience on our package was to ride camels.

We were taken to a nearby collection of camels, and each of us was introduced to a gentle, patient animal waiting calmly in the soft morning light. The camels had big, soulful eyes and long eyelashes—which, when the light hit just right, looked as if they were winking knowingly at us.

Climbing onto a camel was an adventure in itself. With help from the guides, we managed to mount our camels, balancing carefully as we settled into their distinctive, swaying rhythm. The camel ride, unlike the jeep safari, was a slower, more meditative journey.

Riding a crazy camel

I vividly remember the sensation of swaying gently with the camel's every step. It was a peaceful ride; the persistent but soothing creak of the camel's joints, the soft sound of shifting sands under its feet, and the unending expanse of the desert made me feel as if I were in a quiet, timeless world.

Each ride was a cherished moment—a slow, graceful dance with nature's creation.

While the jeep safari filled us with the thrill of speed and the unpredictability of the dunes, the camel ride offered a contrasting calmness. It gave us a chance to observe the desert's subtle beauty: the way the morning light played on the rippled surface of the sand, the distant silhouettes of rocky outcrops, and the occasional gust of wind that sent tiny flurries of sand swirling around.

The camel ride was less about high-speed excitement and more about reflection, a moving meditation on the vastness of the desert and the timeless nature of these magnificent animals.

Our guides shared gentle tales about the history of camel caravans and how these creatures had been the faithful companions of travelers for centuries.

Their stories, told in a careful, enthusiastic tone, added layers of cultural richness to our experience. It was a moment of connection—not just with nature but with the ancient ways of life that had traversed these lands long before us.

With our hearts still exhilarated from the adventures on wheels and on camelback, the day's final chapter awaited us in the cool, enchanted evening.

Our package had included a special cultural event under the open sky—a celebration of Rajasthan's artistic traditions, complete with dance, music, and, of course, songs.

We gathered with other families and guests in an outdoor arena, surrounded by the rustic beauty of the desert at twilight.

As the sun began to set, painting the sky in dramatic hues of red, orange, and purple, a group of local performers took to the stage. The first act was the pot dance—a playful and energetic performance where dancers balanced clay pots on their heads and skillfully moved in synchrony with the upbeat folk tunes.

The dancers, dressed in vibrant traditional attire, twirled and leaped in a joyful display of movement. Their infectious energy immediately drew smiles and applause from our family and the audience alike.

Following the pot dance was the much-anticipated fire dance. Against the backdrop of the darkening sky, dancers wielded controlled flames with breathtaking skill.

The fire shimmered and crackled as the performers moved gracefully, creating mesmerizing patterns in the air. The spectacle was both thrilling and awe-inspiring. The rhythm of the music, the heat of the fire, and the sheer artistry of the performance created an atmosphere of magic that enveloped us all. Between the performances, traditional live songs were sung by local artists using instruments like the dhol, harmonium, and flute.

Their lyrics resonated with the spirit of Rajasthan, inviting us to feel every emotion as we listened. We clapped along, some of us even trying to join in the chorus, letting our voices blend with the melodies under the vast night sky.

The entire cultural event was choreographed to perfection. Every performance had its own story, its own mood, and together they celebrated the rich heritage of Rajasthan in a way that was both fun and deeply moving. It was a reminder that while our day had been filled with outdoor adventures and high-energy rides, the soul of Rajasthan was always in its art, its music, and its dance.

The mesmerizing dances and the fiery spectacle provided a beautiful contrast to the natural adventure of the day—they were like a burst of colors and emotions that completed the portrait of our desert experience.

After the enchanting performances and as the night grew deeper, the grand finale of our desert day arrived—a feast of authentic Rajasthani cuisine. Our package concluded with an elaborate dinner exclusively featuring the famous and traditional flavors of Rajasthan.

We were ushered into a beautifully decorated dining area with low-lit lanterns hanging overhead and traditional Rajasthani decor adorning the walls.

The atmosphere was warm, intimate, and inviting—perfect for sharing a meal with family and new friends made along the way.

The dinner menu was a delightful celebration of Rajasthani flavors. We tasted a variety of dishes that each told its own story. The meal began with a series of freshly made starters, **including kachoris and papadis, along with tangy chutneys that excited the palate.**

For the main course, we feasted on dishes like **dal baati churma**—a hearty combination of lentils, baked wheat balls, and a sweet, crumbly wheat dessert that was divine.

dal baati churma

The rich, aromatic ***gatte ki sabzi***, prepared from gram flour dumplings simmered in a spicy, tangy gravy, added another layer to our culinary adventure.

gatte ki sabzi

Alongside these, we enjoyed **laal maas**—a fiery red meat curry that was as bold in flavor as it was in color—and **ker sangri**, a unique Rajasthani delicacy made with desert beans and dried berries, embodying the rustic charm of the region.

Every bite was a revelation, and as we savored our food, we exchanged stories about the day's adventures and laughed heartily over shared memories. The dinner was served in the traditional thali style, where each dish was arranged on a round platter, allowing us to experience a full spectrum of flavors in one meal. The authenticity of the cuisine, prepared by seasoned local chefs, was evident in every spice and every carefully balanced ingredient.

Sitting together at the long dining table, our family found that the meal was not only a culinary delight but also a fitting end to an exhausting, exhilarating day.

The flavors of the food, the festive atmosphere, and the soft melodies of background music gently fading into the night created a sense of fulfillment and warmth that lingered long after the meal was over.

As the evening drew to a close and we prepared to return to our hotel, I took a few moments to reflect on the day. It had been a day of stark contrasts—from the high-energy thrill of a jeep safari over pulsating sand dunes to the gentle, rhythmic motion of roaming camels.

Each experience was a chapter in our family's desert adventure. The cultural performances filled our hearts with joy, and the authentic Rajasthani feast satisfied our hunger in every way imaginable.

When I went through my photos, I remembered the look of pure joy on my children's faces as they experienced the rugged thrill of riding over the dunes in the jeep and the awe in their eyes as they sat atop a camel, their voices soft with wonder at the endless desert around them.

My sister and I shared quiet smiles, knowing that these were the moments that would become lifelong memories—a tapestry of simple pleasures and grand adventures woven together with love and laughter.

Every detail had contributed to the day's magic. The vibrant colors of the traditional performances, the sound of the drums and the crackling fire during the dance, the gentle rocking of the camel under the endless desert sky, and the comforting familiarity of home waiting at the end of a long day—all of these pieces came together to create an experience that was both exhilarating and deeply calming.

On our ride back to the hotel, our conversations were filled with excited chatter as we tried to recall each detail of what had been the perfect blend of adventure, culture, and cuisine. The memories of the jeep safari and the camel ride kept our spirits buoyant despite the exhaustion that crept into our bodies after a full day.

We knew that these experiences were more than simple activities; they were gateways to understanding a piece of Rajasthan's soul—its traditions, its landscapes, and the resilient spirit of its people.

In those quiet moments on our journey back, as the stars reappeared in the dark desert sky, I felt an overwhelming gratitude for the day's adventures. The entire package had been designed to immerse us in the heart of Rajasthan, and it had done just that. It wasn't just about riding jeep through dunes or sampling fiery curries; it was about experiencing life in its most vibrant forms, shared with the people who mattered most.

By the time we returned to our hotel, we were both tired and filled with a renewed zest for adventure. Our family adventure that day had tested our endurance, expanded our horizons, and brought us closer together through a series of shared experiences.

The sights of the golden dunes, the gentle sway of camels, the vibrant swirl of Rajasthani dance, and the irresistible flavors of our dinner all combined to create a day that would forever be etched in our memories.

Looking back, booking that comprehensive package was one of the best decisions we made during our trip. It allowed us to immerse ourselves entirely in the culture and landscape of Rajasthan, offering a perfect blend of adrenaline-fueled excitement and introspective calm.

Every element—from the thrill of the jeep safari, where the wind rushed past us as we sped over the dunes, to the slow, peaceful camel ride where time seemed to lose all meaning—had its charm.

Then there were the cultural performances: the pot dance, with its elegant balance and playful energy, followed by the dramatic fire dance that lit up the night with its intense beauty, accompanied by soulful songs that resonated deep within our hearts.

And finally, the authentic Rajasthani cuisine—the feast that ended our day was not just a meal; it was the culmination of our journey, a symphony of flavors that told the story of this ancient land.

Today, when I recall that day, I remember the laughter, the shared glances of wonder, and the small moments of togetherness that made everything so special. It wasn't just an adventure in the desert; it was a day of bonding, discovery, and an authentic dive into the rich cultural heritage of Rajasthan. Every moment, from the moment we booked that package to the final bite of our sumptuous thali, reminded us of the beauty of experiencing life with our loved ones by our side.

As our family drifted off to sleep that night, our hearts were full—full of memories and dreams of more adventures to come. That day, woven with the golden threads of adventure, culture, and culinary brilliance, remains a cherished chapter in the story of our travels together.

ppp

This detailed account of our family's desert package adventure—from booking the package to experiencing a heart-racing jeep safari over the sand dunes, a calm and reflective ride atop camels, the mesmerizing power of traditional Rajasthani dances with vibrant songs, and finally a feast showcasing authentic Rajasthani cuisine—captures not just the chronology of events, but the emotions, laughter, and sense of wonder that united us as a family. Every step of that day, every shared glance, and every burst of excitement is now etched in our hearts, a timeless reminder of our journey through the soul of Rajasthan.

As sleep began to lull me into its embrace, a fleeting thought surfaced—a whisper from my heart, reminding me of something precious: my **mom's birthday** was tomorrow.

6

Day 5: Heartfelt Wishes, Celebrations, and Exploring Jaisalmer's Timeless Treasures

In the soft glow of the morning, as the sunlight began to filter through the curtains of our hotel room, I woke up with a special thought in my heart—it was my mom's birthday. My sister, dad, and I quickly gathered around her with wide smiles and warm hugs. It was a tender family moment filled with laughter, affection, and an unspoken promise to make her day truly memorable.

With the birthday wishes and heartfelt moments fresh in our minds, we decided to start the day by indulging in the flavors of Jaisalmer with a local breakfast outing. At around 8:30 a.m., we stepped out into the cool morning air, eager to explore a side of the city that would introduce us to its culinary charms. It wasn't long before we found ourselves in the bustling streets of Jaisalmer, chatting and enjoying hearty breakfasts.

As we saw the local people, we were surprised to see the people eating traditional dishes like Dal Pakwan and Poha listed as breakfast staples—so different from the Dosa and Idli breakfasts we often enjoyed back home in South India. Curious and excited, we decided to try these Rajasthani favorites.

When the plates arrived, they were a feast for the senses. Dal Pakwan, a unique and savory dish, consisted of crispy flatbread served alongside a rich, spiced lentil curry. The pakwan, golden and crunchy, was made with all-purpose flour and fried to perfection, while the dal was a harmonious blend of moong and chana lentils cooked with an aromatic mixture of spices like cumin, coriander, and turmeric. Each bite of the pakwan dipped into the dal was an explosion of textures and flavors—crispy, warm, and deeply satisfying.

Poha, on the other hand, was a lighter yet equally delightful dish. Made from flattened rice, the poha was cooked with mustard seeds, onions, green chilies, and a medley of spices, then topped with fresh coriander leaves and a dash of lemon juice. The soft and fluffy rice absorbed all the flavors, while the tanginess from the lemon added a refreshing twist. Accompanied by crispy sev (fried gram flour strands) sprinkled generously on top, Poha was a simple yet comforting dish that left us feeling energized for the day.

While enjoying these dishes, we couldn't help but compare them to the familiar breakfasts from our region. Where dosas and idlis are typically served with coconut chutneys and sambar, Dal Pakwan and Poha brought to the table a whole new palette of earthy, spicy, and tangy flavors. It was a culinary experience that broadened our perspective and added an extra layer of excitement to the day.

As we enjoyed each bite and soaked in the vibrant atmosphere, we felt grateful for this delicious representation of Jaisalmer's culture served on a plate. The streets buzzed with the laughter of locals and filled the air with the enticing aroma of freshly cooked dishes—creating a moment that made us feel genuinely connected to the heart of the city.

Back at our hotel, Club Mahindra offered a paid tour guide service that provided insights into the history and special features of Jaisalmer Fort. This service also included a personalized birthday cake to celebrate her milestone later in the day, making the occasion joyful and unique, just like the local flavors we had recently discovered. It was a day filled with cultural exploration, heartfelt family moments, and unforgettable experiences—truly a memorable celebration all wrapped into one.

After savoring the flavors of our delightful local breakfast—Dal Pakwan and Poha—on the lively streets of Jaisalmer, we set out to explore one of the city's most iconic landmarks, the Jaisalmer Fort.

The morning air was still cool as we made our way to this colossal structure, often referred to as **Sonar Quila, or the Golden Fort,** because of how its sandstone walls gleam golden under the desert sun. Standing tall amidst the arid landscape, this fort seemed to radiate centuries of history and splendor.

History of Jaisalmer Fort:

Built by Rawal Jaisal, the founder of Jaisalmer, this fort has witnessed the passage of time like a silent storyteller.

Its towering structure, perched atop Trikuta Hill, served as a defense against invasions during the medieval era. Unlike many forts in India, Jaisalmer Fort is unique—it's not just a historical monument but a living fort.

Yes, you read that right! Around **4,000 people** still reside within its fortified walls, making it one of the few forts in the world where life continues in its bustling streets, ancient houses, and myriad shops.

As we entered through one of the massive gateways, the charm of the fort instantly enveloped us. Narrow lanes twisted and turned like a maze, each corner brimming with the hum of life.

Shops selling colorful textiles, intricately embroidered garments, stunning jewelry, and souvenirs lined the streets. The aroma of local snacks wafted through the air as vendors prepared traditional dishes for residents and travelers alike.

The Magnificent Jain Temples:

Exploring deeper into the fort, we arrived at its seven Jain temples, each more captivating than the last. These temples, built between the 12th and 15th centuries, are a visual treat for lovers of architecture. Constructed from yellow sandstone, their walls are adorned with exquisitely carved motifs, intricate patterns, and depictions of Jain Tirthankaras. Their serene ambiance offered a brief respite from the bustling streets outside.

Among these temples, the Chandraprabhu Jain Temple stood out as a marvel. Dedicated to Chandraprabhu, the eighth Jain Tirthankara, this temple mesmerized us with its artistry. The walls of the temple were decorated with intricate carvings that seemed to come alive with every glance. Pillars with detailed floral and geometric patterns supported the structure, each telling a silent story of devotion and craftsmanship.

Chandraprabhu Jain temple

The delicate latticework allowed beams of sunlight to filter in, creating a soft, ethereal glow that heightened the temple's spiritual aura. Standing within this magnificent temple, surrounded by centuries-old artistry, was an experience that left us awestruck and deeply humbled.

Journey to Patwon Ki Haveli:

After thoroughly exploring the fort and soaking in its history and charm, we decided to continue our adventure by visiting another architectural jewel of Jaisalmer—the Patwon Ki Haveli. On our way there, we made a quick stop at Dhanraj Ranmal Bhatia, a famous sweet shop known for its legendary treats.

We couldn't resist indulging in their crispy pyaz kachori, its flavorful onion filling perfectly spiced, and the warm, syrupy jalebis, which were a delightful blend of sweetness and crunch. The culinary stop not only satisfied our taste buds but added another layer of joy to our day. Upon arriving at Patwon Ki Haveli, we were immediately enchanted by its grandeur.

This haveli is not just one building but a cluster of five exquisitely carved mansions, making it the largest haveli in Jaisalmer. It was built by Guman Chand Patwa, a wealthy merchant, in the early 19th century and stands as a testament to the prosperity of the bygone era.

Intricate Artwork on the Patwon Ki Haveli

The beautiful interior of the Haveli

The haveli's architecture is nothing short of breathtaking. The intricate carvings on its yellow sandstone facade seemed to tell tales of opulence and artistry. Balconies and windows adorned with delicate latticework offered a peek into the finesse of the craftsmen who dedicated their skills to this masterpiece. As we wandered through its richly decorated interiors, we were captivated by the elaborate frescoes, antique furniture, and ornate mirrorwork that adorned the walls and ceilings.

Walking through Patwon Ki Haveli, with its towering arches and lavish decor, felt like stepping into a different era—a world where every detail was crafted with precision, beauty, and love. It wasn't just a building; it was a piece of living history, echoing the legacy of the merchants and artisans who once thrived here.

Our exploration of Jaisalmer Fort and Patwon Ki Haveli was a journey through time, blending historical intrigue, artistic marvels, and vibrant local flavors. Each step brought us closer to the soul of Jaisalmer, a city that seamlessly combines the richness of its past with the vibrancy of its present. As we wrapped up our day, the memories of the fort's living streets, the ethereal beauty of Jain temples, and the architectural grandeur of Patwon Ki Haveli stayed with us, leaving us eager to see what more Jaisalmer had in store.

After our delightful exploration of Patwon Ki Haveli, with its intricate carvings and vivid tales of a bygone era etched on every wall, we continued our journey through the enchanting lanes of Jaisalmer. The afternoon sun shone brightly, filling the golden desert city with warmth and a sense of adventure. Our next destination was the famed Bada Bagh, a sprawling garden complex cloaked in history. However, as we inched closer to Bada Bagh, we couldn't help but notice that its grandiosity seemed to diminish with distance.

A Glance at Bada Bagh:

Bada Bagh, known for its royal cenotaphs and memorials dedicated to the rulers of Jaisalmer, lay in the distance like a muted painting. From afar, its appearance was rather unassuming and almost flat, lacking the vibrant energy we had experienced at other monuments. Although the climb to its summit might have offered a closer look at the intricate artistry of the cenotaphs, from our vantage point along the road, it seemed dull and somewhat somber.

After a brief discussion, we decided that given our plans for the day and the limited time we had, it would be best to admire Bada Bagh from a respectful distance. This decision wasn't made lightly; we understood that a rich history thrived within its confines, yet we felt that this was not the right moment for us to explore its quiet narratives. Instead, we left our curiosity at bay, taking in the overall view and snapping a few photos as keepsakes of its understated beauty.

The view was enchanting, with carved memorials against a pale sky, evoking memories of Rajasthan's royal dynasties. Sometimes, a place's splendor is best appreciated from afar, leaving its mysteries intact for future exploration.

A Refreshing Stop at Gadisar Lake:

No sooner had we bid farewell to Bada Bagh than our feet and hearts led us to our next captivating destination: Gadisar Lake. As we approached this serene water body, it became clear that Gadisar Lake was to the city of Jaisalmer what an oasis is to the desert—truly a gem nestled amid the sands. The calm waters mirrored the bright sky above, and the landscape seemed to slow down enough for us to catch our breath, creating a perfect setting for some cherished family moments.

We gathered around the lake's edge, the cool breeze brushing our faces as the gentle ripples on the water's surface fascinated us. It was time for a little fun—a chance to capture some joyful memories. We posed for a series of family selfies, and laughter erupted as we struck spontaneous poses, each expression conveying the pure bliss of being together in such a picturesque environment. The reflective water, fringed by ancient trees and dotted with little boats, provided an idyllic backdrop against which our smiles shone even brighter. Every click of the camera was like freezing a moment of joy, a memory that we knew we'd share and reminisce about for years to come.

Strolling around Gadisar Lake, we took our time to appreciate the gentle interplay of light and shadow on the water, the birds singing overhead, and the serene murmur of water lapping at the banks. The surroundings were inviting and peaceful, a perfect antidote to the sometimes frenetic pace of travel. This brief respite by the lake felt like a mini celebration of our togetherness—a pause to honor the simple yet profound pleasure of family time.

Returning to Club Mahindra Hotel:

Soon, as the day began to wane and the soft hues of the afternoon painted the city in a warm glow, we found ourselves heading back to our home away from home—the Club Mahindra Hotel in Jaisalmer. The journey back was leisurely, our hearts still buoyed by the day's adventures as the taxi meandered through narrow, winding lanes of the old city. Arriving at around 4:00 p.m., the sight of the hotel's majestic facade instantly uplifted our spirits anew.

There was something inherently comforting about the familiar surroundings of our hotel after a day filled with historical explorations and sunlit escapades. Inside, the ambiance of the hotel was warm and inviting. The soft hum of quiet conversations in the lobby and the gentle clink of plates being prepared in the adjacent restaurant signified that it was time to recharge before our next round of fun.

Freshening Up and Heading to the Happy Hub:

After a brief respite in our room, where we took the time to freshen up and regroup, we all felt re-energized and ready for more playful exploration. It was time to visit the Happy Hub—a vibrant recreation area within the hotel renowned for its variety of indoor sports and games and a space that was as spirited as it was welcoming. The Happy Hub was a cheerful oasis designed to offer just the kind of light-hearted amusement that makes travel as enjoyable as it is memorable.

Among the many activities available at the Happy Hub, I found myself drawn most strongly to the air hockey table. With a simple clack of the puck and the constant whoosh of sliding pucks, the game quickly became the centerpiece of our playful competition. The air hockey table was set up in a cozy corner of the hub, with bright neon lights reflecting off its smooth surface, inviting everyone who passed by to take part in the fun. As I challenged my dad and sister in a friendly match, the room filled with laughter and cheers. The playful competition brought us closer together, creating a spirited atmosphere that was both competitive and joyous.

Discovering the Saree Shop at the Happy Hub:

In addition to the air hockey table, the Happy Hub also housed an unexpected treasure—a beautifully curated saree shop. This wasn't just any shop; it was a delightful emporium of color and tradition dedicated to the timeless elegance of Indian sarees and the iconic Rajasthani chuni. The shop's collection was as diverse as it was impressive.

There, alongside the most basic sarees available for modest prices, were also the most intricately designed and richly embellished sarees, priced for those seeking luxury and exclusivity. The range seemed endless—from simple, everyday designs that exuded understated charm to elaborate creations showcasing detailed embroidery, zari work, and vibrant prints that celebrated the opulence of Rajasthan.

As we browsed through the collection, we marveled at how each saree told a story. The lighter, more contemporary pieces seemed to whisper tales of modern fashion intertwined with tradition, while the complex, ornate sarees spoke of heritage, craftsmanship, and an artistry refined over generations. Traditional Rajasthani chunis, with their bright hues and intricate mirror work, hung alongside more conventional sarees, reflecting the dynamic progression of style through the ages in this region. Each piece was meticulously displayed, its rich fabric and detailed patterns a testament to the legacy of Rajasthan's textile art.

We paused, taking in the vibrant display of color and craftsmanship—the very embodiment of the region's culture—and discussed which sarees might make perfect mementos or gifts to cherish.

The atmosphere in the Happy Hub was brimming with light-hearted conversation as we all dipped into our youthful curiosity and engaged in playful banter about styles and patterns. The combination of games, delightful shopping, and a chance to simply unwind created an environment that was vivacious and full of cheer. It was an experience that perfectly encapsulated the multifaceted nature of our day; from historic explorations and serene lakeside selfies to playful competitions and the timeless allure of traditional attire, every moment was underscored by a sense of wonder and joy.

After an eventful day filled with exploration and laughter, our evening began to wind down in the warm, fading light of Jaisalmer. We had just wrapped up an exuberant session at the Happy Hub—a lively space where the cheerful clatter of air hockey, the joy of friendly competition, and the delightful banter of exploring a tiny saree shop had filled our hearts with playful energy. Yet, as the golden afternoon began to melt into a softer dusk, it was time to leave that vibrant haven and retreat to the calm comforts of our room.

Leaving the Happy Hub:
We gathered our belongings and said our temporary goodbyes to the Happy Hub, the laughter still echoing faintly through our ears as we slowly made our way back. Stepping out into the cool evening air, we strolled along the softly lit corridors of the Club Mahindra resort until we reached our room at around 7:30 p.m.

The walk back was quiet and reflective—a gentle transition from the burst of energy at the hub to the peaceful intimacy of our private space. Our room, tastefully decorated with a blend of traditional

Rajasthani accents and modern comforts, was instantly welcoming. The soft lighting, modest furnishings, and the gentle hum of the air conditioner provided a perfect cocoon in which to unwind.

Packing for the Next Adventure:

Once inside, with the door closed against the cool night mist, we set about preparing for our next journey. Our train to Jaipur was slated to depart at 12:30 a.m., and though there were still precious hours left in the evening, we began packing our clothes and essential items.

Everyone participated—with my sister folding her favorite cotton kurta that reminded her of the bright colors of the desert and my dad meticulously checking off the list of travel necessities.

I gathered small mementos from our day, each item a symbol of the vibrant memories we had gathered from Jaisalmer. The process, though mundane, was infused with an unspoken excitement—each article of clothing, each personal care item, was a step closer to our next chapter of adventure.

A Secret Surprise Unfolds:

Amid our packing frenzy, a spark of secret delight shone in my dad's eyes. Unbeknownst to the rest of the family, he had hatched a plan to add a touch of magic to our evening.

Quietly, he slipped away from our room and made his way to the resort's restaurant, a gem within the Club Mahindra complex known for its sumptuous cuisine and warm hospitality.

There, in hushed conversation with the staff, he ordered a beautifully decorated birthday cake for my mom—a surprise to mark the occasion of another year of her grace and kindness. The thoughtfulness of his gesture filled our hearts with anticipation, even as we continued our preparations.

The Birthday Cake Ceremony:

By around 8:30 p.m., our secret had blossomed into an intimate celebration. The cake, arriving shortly after dad's discreet arrangement, was a confectionary masterpiece—its icing swirled like delicate brushstrokes over a canvas of soft sponge, adorned with edible glitters and subtle hints of rose and cardamom.

We gathered in our room, and with a chorus of "Happy Birthday" that was sung with genuine affection and a few playful giggles, we celebrated my mom.

The moment the knife cut through the cake, revealing its moist, fragrant interior, the room was filled with cheers and warm embraces. Each slice we savored was more than just dessert—it was a symbol of love, a silent vow that every milestone in life was to be celebrated with the people who make it all meaningful.

Dinner and a Stroll in the Green Lawn:

Following this tender celebration, our stomachs reminded us that there was still one more delight awaiting that night—a sumptuous dinner at the resort's restaurant. Leaving our room with our hearts light and our spirits high, we made our way to the elegant dining area.

The restaurant was an oasis of soft lights, traditional décor, and modern conveniences, where every table was set to perfection. The menu boasted local Rajasthani specialties, artfully presented and bursting with flavors that paid homage to the rich culinary heritage of the region.

We indulged in a feast that balanced spice and subtlety—a melange of dal, succulent curries, freshly baked bread, tender kebabs, and tangy chutneys that danced on our tongues as much as the cultural notes of the city had danced in our hearts earlier that day. Conversation flowed like the gentle clinking of glasses, and stories from our day at the Happy Hub, the vibrant markets, and our solitary moments at the fort were shared with relish.

After dinner, we felt a pull to step outside and breathe in the cool respite of the resort's outdoor spaces. Hand in hand, we wandered towards the green lawn nestled beside the shimmering pool. Under the expanse of a starlit sky, the lawn, meticulously maintained and soft underfoot, provided the perfect setting for us to linger a while longer.

A soft breeze carried the scent of blooming desert flowers and a faint whisper from the pool's water, creating a serene atmosphere that made the world seem to pause for a moment. We sat together, admiring the tranquility of the space, feeling the cool air brush against our faces, and listening to the gentle murmur of nighttime nature.

Returning to Our Room:

With the night deepening and our minds already turning to the excitement of the upcoming journey, we returned to our room around 10:30 p.m. We gathered our things once again, ensuring every piece was safely tucked into our bags—the birthday cake memory, the echoes of our laughter during dinner, and the whispers of the cool breeze on the green lawn were now all fond imprints on our hearts. The room, softly lit by the dim glow of bedside lamps, welcomed us once more with its quiet tranquility. Here, we took a final look around, savoring our last moments within the cozy cocoon of Club Mahindra.

Final Preparations for the Train Journey:

As the clock inched toward midnight, we resumed our packing with renewed determination. Every piece of our clothing was carefully folded, and every essential item—travel documents, a small first-aid kit, favorite snacks—was checked off in our little mental list one more time.

It was almost surreal how a day of grand explorations, joyful celebrations, and heartfelt surprises could blend seamlessly into the quiet, methodical ritual of packing before a long journey. Yet, every moment was cherished, every step felt significant, and every action was imbued with the warmth of family togetherness.

We could almost taste the anticipation of the next adventure. Our train to Jaipur, scheduled to depart at 12:30 a.m., represented another chapter in our travel narrative—a promise of vibrant bazaars, historical monuments, and stories that were waiting to be unfurled in a city famous for its bustling energy and cultural richness. Even as we carefully arranged our bags near the door, the thought of hordes of travelers, the soft rumble of the train engine, and the gentle lull of a journey filled our hearts with excitement.

A Night of Reflection and Anticipation:

In the quiet of our room, with its soft hum and the gentle ticking of the clock, we sat together for a few moments of reflection. We recounted the day's adventures—from the playful spirit of the Happy Hub to the serene, private celebration of my mom's birthday, from the delectable dinner to the soothing stroll amidst the resort's green lawn.

There was a profound sense of satisfaction in knowing that this day had been a mosaic of magical moments—a day when every laugh, every surprise, and every tender smile had woven together to create memories that would last a lifetime.

As the clock edged closer to midnight, we gave one last look around our room, ensuring all was in order for our departure. With hearts both heavy and buoyant—a blend of melancholy for leaving the resort's gentle embrace and exhilaration for the adventures beyond—we quietly locked our room and prepared to step into the crisp night.

The Final Countdown to Jaipur:

By 12:30 a.m., with our bags neatly slung over our shoulders and the soft light of the night our only companion, we left the resort. The dark sky above seemed endless, a blanket of serenity that promised yet more wondrous experiences in the days to come. Our train to Jaipur awaited us—a vessel not just of transportation but of promise, of stories yet to be written, and of memories yet to be made.

In that final moment before boarding our train, we paused for a heartbeat and shared a collective smile. This journey, with its blend of spontaneous joy and planned surprises, had been a true celebration of life. The surprise birthday cake, the delightful dinner, the gentle caress of the cool breeze on the lawn, and our shared anticipation for the next adventure all mingled together to form a tapestry of perfect moments.

In these few precious hours before our departure, every second was a celebration of togetherness. Our hearts were full, our smiles genuine, and our minds swirled with the joyful memories of the day. With the gentle night winding down and the promise of Jaipur awaiting us, we felt ready—ready to embrace the unknown, to encounter new adventures, and to keep the spirit of our day alive as we traveled onwards, hand in hand, into the night.

As the train slowly pulled out of the station, carrying us away from the warm glow of Club Mahindra, we knew that every goodbye was just a promise of another hello—a promise that our family's journey would continue to be filled with love, laughter, and the many small, unforgettable moments that make travel so magical.

7

Day 6: Arriving in Jaipur

After arriving in the vibrant city of Jaipur and feeling the welcoming pulse of the Pink City, we journeyed to our service apartment, Nimera House—a delightful, elegant abode that immediately felt like a warm embrace after a long day of travel. From the moment we set eyes on its façade, we sensed that here, simplicity and comfort coexisted in a graceful harmony that set it apart from the impersonal ambiance of many famous hotels.

Stepping through the door with anticipation, we were greeted by a spacious layout that unfolded into two serene rooms, a bright and airy hall, and a compact yet well-equipped kitchen. The very design spoke of thoughtful planning—a place where comfort was not sacrificed for luxury, but where both aspects intertwined seamlessly.

Our two rooms served as quiet retreats designed for restful nights after exploring the bustling streets of Jaipur. They were appointed with soft colors and minimalist décor, ensuring that every corner exuded a sense of calm and tranquility.

The natural light that filtered through the windows added an element of warmth, inviting us to relax and let the day's stresses melt away. Each room provided us with a private haven—an intimate space for respite before the adventures of the following day.

The heart of Nimera House, however, was the expansive hall.

This grand yet inviting space was more than just a place to sit; it was a gathering area, a place for conversation, and a venue for sharing memories. A magnificent dining table took center stage, large enough to comfortably seat six people—a feature that was rare when compared to the standard offerings in many hotels.

The table, polished to a gentle shine, promised countless family meals filled with laughter and stories. Around it, two plush, comfortable sofas and a stylish center table created a cozy sitting area where we could unwind while enjoying our favorite TV shows or simply engaging in lively conversation. In this hall, every piece of furniture was arranged with both function and beauty in mind, inviting us to relax completely and feel right at home.

Our journey through Nimera House continued as we explored the kitchen—a small yet highly efficient space that was a testament to simplicity and practicality.

Though modest in size compared to a home kitchen, it was outfitted with all the essentials we needed to prepare our meals. A water purifier stood proudly among the appliances, ensuring that we always had clean, refreshing drinking water at hand. Four stoves were provided, allowing us ample space to cook a variety of dishes using the ingredients we had brought along.

The kitchen's shelves were stocked with spices and other necessary condiments, along with an assortment of glass bowls and plates that promised a delightful dining experience. The setup was straightforward yet effective—a culinary haven that allowed us to create meals and gather around the table with a sense of satisfaction and togetherness.

One of the unique features of Nimera House was its thoughtful approach to bathroom facilities. Unlike many hotels where the bathroom is directly attached to the room, in this apartment, each room was connected to a small adjoining space designed specifically for changing and storing clothes.

This clever arrangement meant that while arriving in or leaving the room, one could do so comfortably in the dedicated space equipped with hangers, perfect for neatly organizing used clothes.

This separation not only enhanced privacy but also contributed to a cleaner, more organized environment overall—a detail that spoke volumes about the care and planning that had gone into designing Nimera House.

Every inch of Nimera House oozed an understated elegance that was both modern and rooted in local aesthetics. The smooth blend of minimalist design with traditional choices created an atmosphere that felt personal and inviting.

The large windows that framed the external views of Jaipur let in not just ample natural light but also provided glimpses of the city's vibrant life outside. At night, the wattage of the soft lighting inside amplified the subtle beauty of the interiors, creating an ambient, almost ethereal, setting that allowed us to unwind completely.

In all, our time at Nimera House was a revelation—a reminder that hospitality can be both luxurious and homely. It provided us with all the comforts we desired: spacious living areas for family bonding, an efficient kitchen for our culinary experiments, neat and practical changing spaces, and an overall ambiance that was both modern and intimately connected with local charm. The service apartment was more than just a temporary lodging; it was a serene retreat that encompassed functionality and elegance, making our stay all the more memorable.

Reflecting on our arrival and settling in, we couldn't help but feel an overwhelming sense of gratitude.

We reached Nimera House at around 2:00 p.m. The sun was high and warm, but the relief we felt upon arriving at our charming retreat was unmistakable. However, there was little time to catch our breath. We quickly dropped our bags, freshened up in our neatly organized changing area, and prepared for our next plan. With a strict departure target of 3:30 p.m., every minute mattered.

Realizing that we needed a hearty, quick lunch, we decided to order from the famed Kanha Restaurant—a local gem recognized for its authentic thali. As we received our order, we were excited by the promise of tasty cuisine. The aroma of spices and freshly cooked food filled the air.

Our thali came laden with small servings of dal, rice, fresh chapati, seasonal vegetables, tangy pickles, and a little dessert to round off the meal. Every little dish on the thali was a delightful discovery—a burst of flavors that spoke of local culinary traditions. Despite our eagerness to savor each bite, we knew we had to keep an eye on the clock. We ate quickly but appreciatively, ensuring no taste was wasted while also keeping our schedule in check.

Our day in Jaipur began with a sense of eager anticipation as we left our service apartment, Nimera House, and set off to explore the historic wonders of the city. The plan was simple and exciting: first, a visit to the majestic Jaigarh Fort, followed by an attempt to reach Nahargarh Fort—also known as the famous Sunset Point—before ending our day with some delightful treats from local culinary gems.

At around mid-afternoon, we piled into the car, our hearts filled with excitement about the day ahead. The drive from our apartment was calm, the streets gradually giving way to the historic outskirts that hinted at the tales of bygone royalty. Our driver navigated through bustling roads and quieter lanes, past neighborhoods echoing decades of tradition, until finally, the mighty Jaigarh Fort came into view.

Jaigarh Fort stood proudly atop a hill, its ancient walls and towering bastions testifying to the might and strategic brilliance of its creators. As we drove up the winding approach, the fort emerged majestically from the red and golden hues of Jaipur's landscape.

Once there, we stepped out of the car with a mix of wonder and excitement. The fort's weathered sandstone walls, the intricate carvings, and the storied corridors all told tales of a time when kings and warriors roamed these lands.

We wandered through the ancient passageways, every step resonating with history. The buildings within the fort had witnessed centuries of battles, royal festivities, and the ebb and flow of life in a vibrant era. The interiors revealed beautiful archways, narrow lanes lined with lattice windows, and rooms that served as silent archives of the past.

We stopped frequently, capturing photographs of every detail that caught our eye: the rounded corners of the arches, the faded patterns on the walls, and the play of light and shadow that lent an almost mystical aura to the space.

One of the highlights of our visit was encountering the legendary Jaivan Cannon. This enormous cannon, mounted on a heavy carriage, loomed large in a corner of the fort. Carefully inscribed with historical details, it narrated in worn-out, elegant script its origin, its role in guarding the fort, and the valor of those who had once wielded its power. According to history, Jaivan is believed to be the largest cannon in the world, which was pulled by elephants and ropes. It can be rotated on a robust four-wheeled carriage with an 8-foot screw to elevate the barrel. Over 100 kilograms of gunpowder was required to fire the Jaivan and marks on the bore through which a 50-kilogram cannonball is fired, indicating that it was not fired more than once. The gun's recoil is about four feet. The Jaivan is also beautifully decorated with auspicious symbols, elephants, and peacocks.

After spending a few precious hours amidst centuries-old relics and architectural marvels at Jaigarh Fort, we reluctantly decided it was time to move on. It was around 5:00 p.m. when we left the fort, our hearts still buzzing with stories and images of battles, celebrations, and daily life from centuries past. Our next destination was Nahargarh Fort, known widely as Sunset Point.

This fort, perched at a slightly lower elevation, was famed for offering splendid views of the city bathed in the golden light of dusk.

However, our journey toward Nahargarh was not without obstacles. The roads leading there were teeming with traffic, and despite a lively conversation and a hopeful spirit, we found ourselves stuck in a slow-moving line of vehicles for nearly an hour.

The minutes dripped away, and soon enough, we realized with regret that the much-anticipated sunset had already passed. The vibrant hues of the sky—the brilliant oranges, pinks, and purples that one expects to see while watching the sun dip below Jaipur's skyline—were now nothing but a memory. With heavy hearts, we conceded that today was not the day for a visit to Nahargarh Fort. The picturesque view we had hoped to witness was lost to time and traffic.

Yet, even in disappointment, Jaipur had delightful surprises in store. Our ever-resourceful driver, well-versed in the local treasures, recommended a visit to a famous local sweet and snack shop: Rawat Misthan Bhandar. As we made our way out of the traffic, the aroma of fried delicacies and sweet syrups soon enveloped us. The shop was bustling, with locals and visitors alike eagerly lining up for their share of culinary delights.

At Rawat Misthan Bhandar, we decided to try the much-raved-about pyaz kachori. As soon as the steaming plate was placed before us, a burst of flavors greeted our senses. The kachori was golden and perfectly crisp on the outside, generously stuffed with a spicy, tangy onion filling that was the very best we had ever tasted. It was wonderfully spicy yet balanced, with just the right crunch. Alongside the kachoris, our feast extended to a plate of jalebis, ghevar, and pani puri. The jalebi was exquisitely crispy—delicately sweet yet with a subtle hint of tartness that made every bite just as delightful as the last. The ghevar, with its airy texture and lightly sweet flavor, was a tribute to traditional Rajasthani sweets. And the pani puri offered a playful, tangy twist with its burst of mint and spice, leaving a refreshing zing on the palate.

As we concluded our indulgent mini-feast at Rawat Misthan Bhandar, our driver, with a twinkle of excitement in his eyes, suggested one more stop—a visit to the renowned chai shop, Gulab Ji Chai Wale. This chai shop was a local favorite, a bustling haven of warm chai, delectable fast food, and vibrant chatter.

Arriving at Gulab Ji Chai Wale, we noticed the shop was teeming with people. Locals and travelers mingled together, enjoying the inviting warmth and the bustling energy that marked this humble yet celebrated establishment.

We stepped inside, and the inviting scent of freshly brewed tea immediately wrapped around us like a comforting blanket. Besides its famed chai, the shop's menu boasted a fascinating array of delicacies beyond the ordinary.

There was chowmein, noodles, and an assortment of other fast food items that added a modern twist to the traditional fare.

Still, it was the chai that called out to us. With its robust aroma, perfectly balanced with a hint of spice and a touch of sweetness, every sip felt as if we were embracing the spirit of the city in a warm cup. The chai was prepared with care, its consistency the perfect blend of bold and mellow flavors—a truly heartwarming experience that left us feeling refreshed and slightly invigorated after the long day.

After finishing our delightful chai and fast-food fix at Gulab Ji Chai Wale around 8:30 p.m., we decided that our adventure wasn't over yet. With laughter still echoing in our ears from the earlier bustling chai shop, we hopped into our car and set course for Nehru Bazaar. Now, if you haven't been to Nehru Bazaar in Jaipur, let me tell you—it's a vibrant microcosm of the city itself, a place where the art of bargaining meets the magic of discovering hidden treasures.

The sole purpose of Nehru Bazaar is more than just commerce. It is a meeting point, a social hub where locals and tourists alike come together to explore, buy, and share stories. Unlike the other grand bazaars of Jaipur, such as Johari Bazaar—where you can find dazzling jewelry- or Bapu Bazaar—with its riot of textiles and handicrafts, Nehru Bazaar is a little more laid-back and quirky. It is a marketplace dedicated to everyday charm, where you can see the pulse of Jaipur in every colorful stall and every friendly smile.

Here, the stalls display everything from footwear, bags, garments, and textiles to unverifiable "one-of-a-kind" treasures that make you chuckle just at the thought of their origin. As we strolled through the narrow lanes, our eyes darted excitedly between the beautifully embroidered fabrics and the rustic leather sandals—yes, these sandals were so boldly displayed that one vendor even claimed they could "conquer the world" if you gave them a try! We couldn't help but laugh at his theatrical sales pitch, which was as colorful and spirited as the items he was selling.

Every shop at Nehru Bazaar was like a mini-adventure. One stall showcased an eclectic mix of footwear in every shade and style imaginable—from elegant juttis that looked as if they'd danced off the pages of a folklore to sturdy, retro boots that made our feet tap with delight. In another corner, a collection of bags in myriad textures—from soft leather to handwoven fabrics—sat atop makeshift displays, inviting us to run our fingers along their intricate designs.

As we ambled further along the bustling thoroughfare, our attention was caught by a shop brimming with garments and textiles. Here, the vibrancy of Jaipur was stitched into every piece: rich, saturated colors, intricate patterns, and a variety of styles meant for every kind of celebration. We marveled at the remarkable craftsmanship and even tried on a few pieces for laughs. My sister found herself twirling in an intricately designed dupatta, while Dad playfully donned a quirky turban that made us all chuckle. The ambiance was lighthearted and fun—a perfect blend of commerce and comedy.

The charm of Nehru Bazaar wasn't just in the items but in the energy of the place. Bargaining here was an art form, and though some negotiations turned into playful banter rather than fierce haggling, every moment felt like contributing to an age-old tradition.

Vendors, with their smiling faces and animated gestures, told stories about the origins of their merchandise and sometimes even recited little jokes that brightened the air even further. Their enthusiasm was infectious, and we found ourselves swept up in the communal excitement of the market vibe.

All this hustle and bustle, combined with a delightful dose of Jaipur's infamous bargaining theater, led us into a joyous trance. It wasn't long before we discovered, quite humorously, that time had danced away with us. The sun had already bid farewell, and the cool night had wrapped the city in a silken darkness.

Our shopping bags were heavy with quirky finds—from a pair of boldly patterned shoes meant "to conquer the world" to intricately woven scarves and embroidered chudidars. We left the bazaar with smiles, our hearts and hands full of souvenirs that we knew would spark conversations (and chuckles) back home.

Eventually, in true Jaipur style, we navigated the late-night streets back to our service apartment, Nimera House. The drive was leisurely yet filled with snippets of conversation, punctuated by laughter over the amusing sales pitches we'd encountered earlier. As we finally pulled up to Nimera House, it was already quite late, but our tiredness was washed away by the thrill of the day's adventures.

Inside our charming apartment, the elegant décor and warm ambiance of Nimera House welcomed us home. Despite the exhaustion, our spirits were high, and we shared our favorite moments of the night—especially that one vendor's audacious claim about his sandals and the playful banter over colorful textiles. Each item we'd bought was a delightful reminder of our escapade, and we knew that they would soon adorn our shelves and closets, carrying with them the unforgettable energy of Nehru Bazaar.

In retrospect, our impromptu visit to Nehru Bazaar turned out to be the perfect end note to a day filled with history and flavor. It was a space where the exuberance of Jaipur's everyday life came alive in a symphony of colors, playful negotiations, and genuine smiles. And even though we returned back to our comfortable Nimera House a little later than planned, the joy we carried with us made every minute of the late return worth it.

Thus, as we settled in for the night, surrounded by the thoughtful details of our service apartment and the soft hum of the city outside, our hearts were light, our laughter shared, and our memories enriched by the magic—and misadventures—of Nehru Bazaar.

8

Final Rush Through Jaipur: Unseen Wonders and a Heartfelt Goodbye

Our day in Jaipur began with a palpable sense of adventure and wonder as we set out early to explore one of the city's most iconic landmarks—Amer Fort. The majestic ramparts of Amer Fort rose before us like echoes from a regal past, their sandstone walls bathed in the soft glow of the morning sun. As we walked through the expansive courtyard, every intricate carving and ornate window spoke of a history filled with valor, romance, and artistry. We couldn't resist capturing every moment; our cameras clicked continuously, preserving the timeless beauty of this historic marvel.

Inside the fort, we first visited the Amber Palace, where the fusion of Mughal grandeur and Rajput valour was evident in every detail of its architecture. The airy chambers with their high arched ceilings, delicately carved pillars, and expansive, intricately patterned courtyards left us in awe. Every wall seemed to narrate stories of a bygone era, and we took what felt like millions of photos, determined to remember each ornate detail and every vibrant hue that adorned the palace's interior.

Our journey inside Amer Fort continued as we made our way to the renowned Sheesh Mahal, or Mirror Palace. This part of the fort was a dazzling display of glass and mirror work—the walls shone brilliantly as if sprinkled with stardust, reflecting light in countless mesmerizing patterns. We couldn't help but strike poses for selfies and group photos against this shimmering backdrop, our smiles mirroring the ornate beauty surrounding us. Each beam of light that danced on the polished surfaces deepened our appreciation for the remarkable craftsmanship of those who had built this wonder.

After spending a memorable morning soaking in the splendor of Amer Fort, we hopped into a jeep for a short yet equally fascinating trip to the Amer Stepwell. The stepwell, a marvel of ancient water architecture, was a cool retreat from the desert heat. As we descended its steps, intricately carved with motifs that told tales of the past, I marveled at the ingenuity of creating such a reservoir. Its descending levels, lined with delicate stone railings and artistic reliefs, made it seem like a staircase leading into an enchanted underground world. We took our time to capture the play of shadow and light among the steps, each click of the camera adding another fragment to our growing tapestry of Jaipur memories.

Following the stepwell visit, our journey led us to the UNESCO World Heritage site of Jantar Mantar—a realm where science meets art most fascinatingly. The vast complex of astronomical instruments left me both excited and humbled by the genius of ancient astronomers.

Here, we marveled at the enormous Samrat Yantra, a giant sundial that not only kept time but was an exquisite blend of precision and beauty in stone. Beside it stood the Jai Prakash Yantra, designed to measure the altitude and declination of celestial bodies, among other instruments that revealed the secrets of our solar system. Each device was a testament to the scientific curiosity and brilliance of the past, and the fact that Jantar Mantar was recognized as a UNESCO World Heritage site filled me with immense pride and excitement. There are many other things which are present in Jantar Mantar, but I don't want to bore you, and neither do I want to bore myself by gathering that information.

Examples of some architectural masterpieces usually related to celestial bodies

Our day's exploration of Jaipur eventually drew us towards its famed Hawa Mahal as we neared the end of our journey in Rajasthan. We approached this "Palace of Winds" with eager anticipation, its iconic facade of hundreds of small windows creating a visual spectacle under the soft glow of late afternoon light. Although we only admired the Hawa Mahal from the outside—capturing its picturesque beauty in photos rather than venturing inside—we were content with the perfection of its exterior design. The delicate lattice work, the grandeur of its pink sandstone façade, and the stories embedded in its history spoke volumes, even from a distance.

Hawa Mahal

As the day drew to a close, my heart was filled with a heady mix of exhilaration and a touch of sadness. The excitement of exploring such incredible monuments, the thrill of snapping countless photos of the ornate Amer Fort and the dazzling Sheesh Mahal, and the intellectual wonder sparked in the presence of Jantar Mantar had all culminated into one unforgettable day. Yet, as we prepared to leave Jaipur, there was a bittersweet feeling in the air—a gentle sadness knowing that our adventure in this magical city, and indeed in all of Rajasthan, was drawing to an end.

Driving away from Hawa Mahal, with the soft evening light painting the city in hues of gold and pink, I couldn't help but reflect on the vivid moments of the day. Every landmark we visited, every burst of laughter captured in a selfie, and every historical tale we learned had enriched our journey. Though a day filled with majestic forts, intricate architecture, and scientific marvels finally came to a close, the memories of Jaipur's splendor and the legacy of Rajasthan will forever shine brightly in my heart.

A Timeless Farewell And The Promise Of Tomorrow

As I close this book of wanderlust, my mind overflows with memories of a truly marvelous trip through Rajasthan—where every city painted its enchanting tale, and every moment was a mix of awe, laughter, and a dash of quirky adventure.

In Udaipur, I marveled at royal palaces and serene lakes that glimmered like a painter's palette. The City Palace and Bagore Ki Haveli transported me back in time, with every intricate carving and graceful arch narrating stories of regal splendor. I still chuckle remembering how even the water droplets on Fateh Sagar Lake seemed to dance in celebration of history and art!

Moving on to Jaisalmer, the golden city of deserts, I found myself lost in an ocean of sun-kissed sands and stellar forts. Jaisalmer Fort, with its timeless charm and narrow, bustling lanes, felt alive as ever, and I couldn't resist capturing countless snapshots—each one overflowing with vibrant colors and the quirky energy of a live-in museum. Even Patwon Ki Haveli, with its opulent architecture and secret corners, turned into a stage for spontaneous selfies and playful laughter. Who knew ancient artifacts could be so photogenic and so humbly hilarious?

Then there was Jaipur, where the day began amidst the noble splendor of Amer Fort. The majestic Amber Palace, the dazzling Sheesh Mahal with its mirror magic, and the intriguing stepwells crafted a journey that was as epic as it was Instagram-worthy.

At Jantar Mantar, I found myself awestruck by astronomical instruments like the Samrat Yantra—a sundial that could probably tell more secrets than my best friend—and other contraptions that demystified the cosmos. And although Hawa Mahal beckoned with its delicate latticed beauty, we decided to simply admire it from the outside, saving our adventurous spirits for moments that truly wove our hearts into Jaipur's history.

Now, as a new chapter beckons with my move into 11th and 12th classes, I realize that this trip was not just a vacation—it was a memorable turning point in my life. Much like the majestic forts and intricate palaces I explored, the coming years will be built on hard work, resilience, and the courage to explore uncharted territories.

Every step, photo, and shared laugh on this journey reminds me that life is precious, unpredictable, and infinitely beautiful—even if it sometimes means getting a bit lost in traffic or missing out on a sunset. And although I now say a heartfelt goodbye to the magic of Rajasthan, I carry its spirit with me, fueling my ambitions and lighting up my future endeavors.

Here's to the unforgettable memories and to the hilarity, and hard work that lie ahead—a grand farewell and a hilarious hello to the new adventures that await!